THE LOUISIANA PURCHASE

In 1803 President Thomas Jefferson opened negotiations with France to buy the port of New Orleans. Instead, Napoleon Bonaparte offered for sale *all* Louisiana, an area equal in size to the United States as it was then — and even today equal to about a third of the country. Jefferson decided to buy it without referring the matter to the individual states. It was the greatest exercise of federal authority up to that time and one that marked the start of growing federal power. New England objected, fearing that its agrarian rivals, the South and West, would expand into the new territory and grow stronger than the mercantile North. And the extreme Federalists even threatened secession. Plots also developed to separate the western states and territories, including the Louisiana Purchase, from the United States. But most of the nation favored its acquisition, and as the reports of the first explorers were published, Americans for the first time knew what lay west of them.

PRINCIPALS

THOMAS JEFFERSON (1743-1826), third president of the United States, 1801-09.

NAPOLEON BONAPARTE (1769-1821), first consul of France, 1799-1804; emperor, 1804-14.

ROBERT R. LIVINGSTON (1746-1813), United States minister to France who negotiated the purchase of Louisiana.

AARON BURR (1756-1836), vice president of the United States, 1801-05. In 1805 he left the vice presidency and became involved in plots to separate the western states and territories, including the Louisiana Purchase, from the United States.

JAMES WILKINSON (1757-1825), brigadier general, Commander-in-Chief of the United States Army, 1796-1809. Associated with Burr's intrigue, he later denounced him and became a witness against him.

MERIWETHER LEWIS (1774-1809), captain in United States Army; in 1801-03 President Jefferson's private secretary. With William Clark he led an expedition to explore the Louisiana Purchase, 1804-06.

WILLIAM CLARK (1770-1838), frontiersman, co-leader of the Lewis and Clark Expedition.

ZEBULON MONTGOMERY PIKE (1779-1813), lieutenant in the United States Army, leader of an expedition into the southwestern part of the Louisiana Purchase in 1806-07.

A United States commander receives the transfer of Upper Louisiana from the French at St. Louis. Painting by Alfred Russell.

A FOCUS BOOK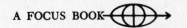

The Louisiana Purchase, April 30, 1803

*Thomas Jefferson
Doubles the Area of
the United States*

by James P. Barry

FRANKLIN WATTS, INC.
NEW YORK/1973

*The authors and publisher of the Focus Books wish
to acknowledge the helpful editorial suggestions of
Professor Richard B. Morris*

Map by Walter Hortens

Photographs courtesy of:
Library of Congress: p. 14; Library, The State Historical Society of Colorado: p. 68 (top); New York Public Library Picture Collection: pp. ii, vi, 12, 23, 32, 39,
42, 48, 53, 59, 68 (bottom), 76; Perry Pictures: pp. 11,
18; State Historical Society of Wisconsin: pp. 35, 46
(top and bottom)

Library of Congress Cataloging in Publication Data

Barry, James P.
    The Louisiana Purchase, April 30, 1803.

    (A Focus book)
    SUMMARY: Chronicles the events which led to
Jefferson's acquisition of Louisiana from Napoleon
Bonaparte.
    Bibliography: p.
    1. Louisiana Purchase—Juvenile literature. [1. Loui-
siana Purchase] I. Title.
E333.B3   973.4'6   72-6836
ISBN 0-531-02460-1

Contents

The Decision to Sell

Napoleon Bonaparte, first consul of France, reclined in his bath at the Palace of the Tuileries in Paris. He was a small man with fine, almost effeminate features. It was the morning of April 7, 1803. The thirty-four-year-old Napoleon would not become emperor until 1804, but already he was in absolute control of his country.

Robert R. Livingston, United States minister to France, had written to Secretary of State James Madison, "There never was a Government in which less could be done by negotiation than here. There is [sic] no people, no Legislature, no counselors. One man is everything. He seldom asks advice, and never hears it unasked. His Ministers are mere clerks; and his Legislature and counselors parade officers."

The first consul's bath resembled a swimming pool more than a tub. As he lay in the perfumed water, there was a scratching at the door like that of a cat; Napoleon had directed a few weeks before that this form of announcement be used in the palace rather than knocking. His younger brother Lucien was ushered in and Napoleon greeted him pleasantly, commenting that he was sorry Lucien had not been able to attend the opera with him the previous evening.

They talked for some time and Napoleon was about ready to leave the bath when the scratching was repeated. A servant brought in Napoleon's older brother, Joseph, and the bather settled back into the water, saying that he would stay there another quarter of an hour. He turned to Joseph and asked if he had spoken to Lucien

Napoleon Bonaparte, as painted by Antoine Gros, after his victory at Arcola.

about their plan for Louisiana. Joseph protested that it was not *his* plan; and some lengthy bickering followed between the two of them.

"Lucien," Napoleon said then, "I have decided to sell Louisiana to the Americans."

Lucien hesitated; he had made the treaty by which Spain recently had returned Louisiana to France, and he was proud of that effort. Then he said that he agreed with Joseph that the Chambers — the legislature — would never consent to the sale.

Napoleon's anger boiled up and he announced that he had no intention of referring the matter to the Chambers. A violent argument followed as to whether or not Louisiana should be sold. The argument contained more emotion than reason; Joseph, his face scarlet, stooped over the bath, screaming at Napoleon who, by contrast, had grown white with anger. The first consul rose up in the bath, then dropped back into it, sending a fountain of water over Joseph and soaking his clothing.

The valet, who until recently had been employed by Joseph, hurried to help the elder brother and tried to dry him off. But the terrifying spectacle of the absolute and often ruthless dictator quarreling with his brothers was too much, and the servant dropped to the floor in a faint.

That ended that argument. Joseph picked up the man and Lucien rang for help. Other servants came quickly and at Napoleon's direction carried the valet away and cared for him.

A sullen Joseph went home to change his clothing while Lucien waited half an hour for Napoleon to dress and then resumed the discussion in the first consul's office. Napoleon, again in a friendly mood, explained why he was going to sell Louisiana. The British navy for a long time to come would be superior to the French navy, and that would make it difficult in case of war for France to hold her overseas possessions. Louisiana would be one of the first areas the British would capture. Moreover, France needed money for the wars that Napoleon saw coming.

Lucien still did not agree. He protested that it would be more honorable to keep their promise to Spain and not sell Louisiana, and that the sale without reference to the Chambers was "too unconstitutional."

This led to another violent argument, and Lucien finally backed cautiously away from his brother and left him in his office.

The Territory
of Louisiana

At the beginning of the nineteenth century Louisiana was a wide and vaguely defined territory covering not only most of present-day Louisiana but also part or all of Texas, Oklahoma, Arkansas, Missouri, Kansas, Colorado, Nebraska, Iowa, Minnesota, North and South Dakota, Wyoming, and Montana. It was roughly a third of the area that today makes up the United States; generally, though not precisely, it was what today we think of as the western part of the Mississippi Valley.

The region had had a long history. It was explored first by the Frenchman Robert Cavelier, Sieur de la Salle, who claimed it for King Louis XIV on April 9, 1682. The French continued to hold it and in 1700 built a small fort on the Mississippi about thirty miles below present-day New Orleans. The little settlement struggled on for a number of years under a succession of officials, some good and some bad. After the death of Louis XIV, the Duke of Orléans became regent for the five-year-old Louis XV. A tremendous public debt of the French royal treasury had been built up by the extravagances of Louis XIV. This debt was now being imposed upon the people of France in the form of heavy taxes. The Duke of Orléans and the Scotsman John Law, a brilliant but unscrupulous financial wizard, decided on a scheme to pay off the debt.

In 1717 a private company that for four years had undertaken to make a commercial success out of the Louisiana colony gave up its charter in disgust. With the Duke of Orléans's approval, John Law then formed the Company of the West, which was given a complete monopoly on the commerce of Louisiana for twenty-five years. Through wide publicity, Law whipped up

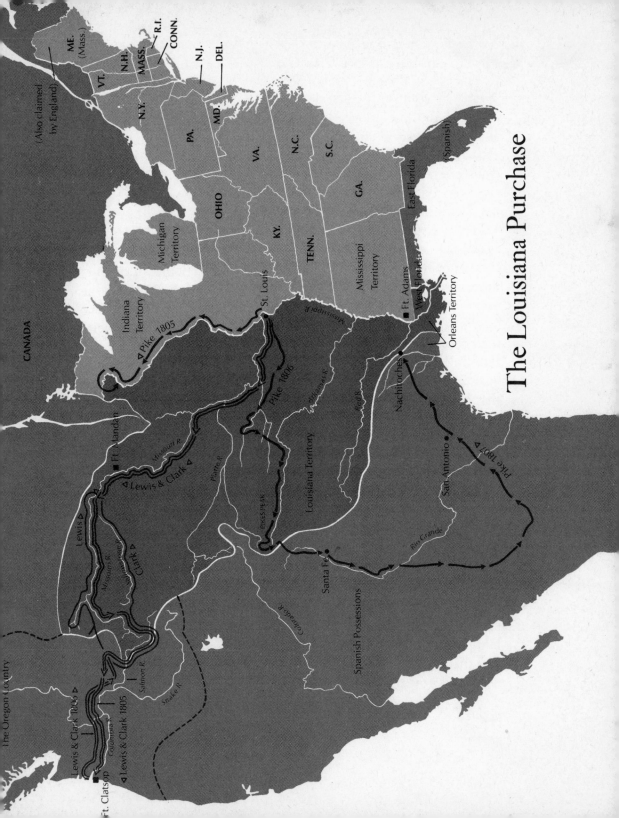

The Louisiana Purchase

CANADA

(Also claimed by England)

ME. (Mass.)

N.H.

VT.

MASS.

R.I.

CONN.

N.Y.

N.J.

DEL.

PA.

MD.

VA.

N.C.

S.C.

GA.

OHIO

Michigan Territory

Indiana Territory

KY.

TENN.

Mississippi Territory

East Florida (Spanish)

West Florida

Ft. Adams

Orleans Territory

St. Louis

Pike 1805

Mississippi R.

Arkansas R.

Red R.

Nachitoches

San Antonio

Pike 1807

Louisiana Territory

Pike 1806

Pikes Peak

Santa Fe

Rio Grande

Spanish Possessions

Ft. Mandan

Missouri R.

Lewis & Clark

Platte R.

Lewis

Clark

Missouri R.

Yellowstone R.

Colorado R.

The Oregon Country

Ft. Clatsop

Lewis & Clark 1806

Lewis & Clark 1805

Columbia R.

Salmon R.

Snake R.

great interest in his company. Among his selling points were the value of the gold, silver, and precious stones that — according to him — were abundant in the distant territory. Frenchmen eagerly bid for shares in the company, and soon the value of the stock rose wildly.

The duke then made Law's private bank, which backed the company, into a government institution, the Royal Bank, so that France itself would share in the profits. There followed mergers with the Company of East India and the Company of China, other French colonial companies. The name of the combined firm then become the Company of the Indies. In addition to running his giant company, Law became comptroller-general of France. But in 1720 the "Mississippi Bubble" — as the celebrated financial scheme came to be called — exploded. There was a run on the Royal Bank and Law had to flee the country. These developments gave most Frenchmen a very unfavorable opinion of Louisiana that lasted for many years afterward.

By this time, the towns of New Orleans and Natchez had been settled, but the Louisiana colony as a whole remained badly governed and torn by petty squabbles. At the end of the Seven Years' War (and its North American campaigns, the French and Indian Wars), France had lost Canada and all holdings east of the Mississippi River except New Orleans. As a result of the Mississippi Bubble, France had little affection for the remaining colony, and having lost everything else in North America she determined to give up Louisiana as well. Louis XV presented it to his somewhat reluctant cousin, Charles III of Spain, who probably accepted it only because it would provide a buffer between the English colonies in North America and Spanish Mexico. The small importance that the great powers gave to the colony is shown by the fact that although France officially gave it up in 1762, the actual change of government did not take place until 1769.

The Spanish regime generally preserved French customs and laws, and under it the morale of the colony improved. Some of the Acadians — French people who had been expelled by the English from present-day Nova Scotia — had drifted down into Louisiana of their own accord. The Spanish decided to bring there three thousand additional Acadian refugees who were then living a hand-to-mouth existence in France. Spain, France, and the refugees already settled in the colony cooperated to settle these additional Acadians, who soon formed a solid group of citizens.

The Right of Deposit

New Orleans began to assume great importance to the interior United States, that part of the new nation developing along the Ohio River. The American settlers living there floated their products in boats down the Ohio and Mississippi rivers to New Orleans. In 1795 the Treaty of San Lorenzo provided that for three years the Americans could "use the port of New Orleans as a place of deposit for their produce and merchandise, and to export the same free of all duty or charge, except a reasonable consideration to be paid for storage and other incidental expenses."

But by secret treaty on October 1, 1800, Spain, under French pressure, returned the Louisiana colony to France, now headed by First Consul Napoleon Bonaparte who was planning his wars of European conquest. The French agreed that they would never cede the territory to a third party. This point was insisted upon by the Spaniards in order to maintain the buffer between the growing United States and Spain's Mexican holdings. When the treaty became general knowledge in 1801, the United States, which had been finding postrevolutionary France increasingly hard to deal with, became acutely concerned. Now France, the greatest military power in history up to that time, and under the leadership of a dictator bent on conquest, was established on the western frontier of the United States. In 1802 the government of Louisiana canceled the right of deposit at New Orleans — it had been permitted to continue well beyond the three years originally specified. The interior United States was thrown into an uproar; how were the settlers to get their products to market?

Bonaparte's first plan for Louisiana was to turn it into a military base by occupying it with a sizable expedition. He could then attack British holdings in Canada and through military pressure control the United States. But instead, the first army destined for Louisiana had to be drawn off regiment by regiment and sent to San Domingo to regain that island from its black inhabitants. However, Napoleon's attempts were frustrated by a combination of yellow fever and guerrilla warfare. Again Napoleon gathered troops and supplies at Belgian and Dutch ports, but heavy winter freezes early in 1803 held up that expedition when the ships became locked in the ice. By the spring thaw, British warships were blockading the Channel and North Sea ports, and the French expedition had to be canceled.

President Jefferson
Looks Westward

Thomas Jefferson was inaugurated third President of the United States in 1801. A month before his inauguration he had asked Meriwether Lewis, a family friend and a captain in the First United States Infantry, to become his private secretary. Among Jefferson's other acquaintances there were many men who would have made better secretaries. The captain seems to have been chosen for quite another reason than his clerical abilities. For a number of years Jefferson had been looking westward; as secretary of state, he had said that in case of war the United States would have to seize Louisana. He knew that there was a common opinion among the foreign ministries of Europe that the United States, unless it was utterly defeated or dismembered, would in time expand across the Mississippi, and that seems also to have been his own opinion. The President intended to send an expedition into the far western area at the earliest possible time, and Captain Lewis was the ideal man to lead it.

On January 18, 1803, Jefferson sent a secret message to Congress asking for $2,500 to finance an expedition that would ascend the Missouri River to its source and go on from there to the Pacific Coast. Publicly, the expedition would be announced as "a literary pursuit," that is, an endeavor to gain geographic and scientific information. But in addition it would have the unannounced purpose of developing the fur trade among the Indians of the upper Missouri and those farther north, and of diverting as much of that trade as possible from Canada down the Missouri to the United States.

Thomas Jefferson, third president of the United States.

[10]

Thus the President was proposing an expedition through territory that belonged to France, in order to draw away the main business of the British holding in Canada. In addition, the expedition was to discover the best route to what later would be called Oregon, an area to which the United States laid claim and with which it had developed an ocean-borne trade in sea-otter furs. The Canadian fur traders were also known to be pushing westward, trying to find an overland route to the Pacific. The trip by sailing ship around Cape Horn was long and difficult. An overland route would have many advantages for whoever discovered it first. But obviously it would have those advantages only if it was *not* in foreign territory. At that time, Jefferson could not know how the United States would gain the lands to its west, but he clearly felt that in time it would own them.

The Charles Willson Peale portrait of Meriwether Lewis, who, with William Clark, explored Louisiana and the far northwest in 1804–06.

The Move to
Buy New Orleans

As a result of the cancellation of the right of deposit at New Orleans, President Jefferson decided that he would try to buy that city. The Senate approved the idea by a bare margin, 15 to 12, and Jefferson appointed James Monroe as "Minister Extraordinary and Plenipotentiary" to France to negotiate the purchase. This was a dramatic move intended mainly to keep the westerners quiet for a time; Jefferson feared that otherwise they might descend upon New Orleans and seize it, thereby precipitating the United States squarely into the Napoleonic wars. The purchase of New Orleans would also be the first step toward accomplishment of Jefferson's larger dream — acquisition of all Louisiana.

Robert Livingston, the United States minister then in France, was not pleased at the appointment of Monroe. For some time he himself had been trying to get the French to negotiate the sale of New Orleans. As early as January of 1803 he had urged Charles Talleyrand-Périgord, Napoleon's minister of foreign affairs, to sell New Orleans, but Talleyrand was evasive. Upon hearing of Monroe's appointment, Livingston wrote to Secretary of State Madison, "I cannot but wish, sir, that my fellow-citizens should not be led to believe, from Mr. Monroe's appointment, that I had been negligent of their interests, or too delicate on any of the great points intrusted to my care."

Robert R. Livingston, minister to France during the Louisiana Purchase.

Napoleon Responds

On April 11, 1803, at daybreak, Napoleon called his treasury minister, François Barbé-Marbois, to him. He showed him reports that the British were arming, but even so he announced that he intended to carry out his own aims in Europe. He went on,

> *I renounce Louisiana. It is not only New Orleans that I wish to cede, it is the whole colony, without reserving anything of it. . . . To insist upon its preservation would be madness. . . . I direct you to negotiate this affair with the envoys of Congress. Do not even wait for the arrival of Mr. Monroe; have an interview this very day with Mr. Livingston. But I have need of a great deal of money for this war, and I should not like to begin it with new contributions. For a hundred years France and Spain have been incurring expenses for improvements in Louisiana, whose trade has never repaid them. . . . But remember this well; I want fifty millions, and for less than this amount I shall not treat. I would rather make a desperate attempt to keep those beautiful countries.*

The two men went on to discuss the rights of sovereignty, and Marbois raised the problem of, in effect, selling the inhabitants of the area. Napoleon brushed this aside, but the comments seem to have made some impression on him. Later Napoleon insisted that the treaty include the stipulation that the inhabitants would have the rights of American citizens.

The first consul did not want the negotiations known to the British until they were completed. "Observe the greatest secrecy," he told his minister, "and recommend it to the American ministers; they have no less interest in it than you." He also instructed Marbois to keep Talleyrand informed of his progress. The minister then withdrew to make his plans.

Negotiations Begin

Later that same day, Livingston was encouraged when Talleyrand suddenly asked him if the United States might want to buy *all* Louisiana.

Livingston responded that the United States was only interested in New Orleans. Talleyrand's answer to this was that if the French gave up New Orleans, they would have little use for the remainder. Livingston agreed; perhaps, he said, the United States might pay twenty million francs for the lot. The French minister countered that the offer was much too low, and suggested that Livingston think about it and discuss the matter further with him at a later time.

Thus Livingston had laid all the groundwork when Monroe arrived on April 13. He dutifully gave a small dinner party for the new minister that evening, but he must have felt that Monroe had come just in time to pluck the fruit that he had carefully nurtured.

Monroe, for his part, seemed to resent Livingston's having done anything at all before he got there. In his first report to Madison he said of Livingston, "His official correspondence will show what occurred prior to my arrival and sufficiently proves that he did not abstain even on learning that I was on my way, from the topics intrusted to us jointly," and he continued with a number of petty complaints about his host.

During the dinner Livingston noticed with some surprise that Barbé-Marbois was walking outside in the garden. He sent out to invite him to join the party, but Marbois declined, saying that he would return after they had dined. While the group was drinking its after-dinner coffee, he joined them. In time he and Livingston had the opportunity to stroll together into the next room and be

by themselves. After some brief talk, Marbois said that he had an important matter to discuss, but that as Livingston's house was full of company it would be better if the American minister called on him later that evening. He then excused himself.

As soon as his guests had departed, Livingston went to Barbé-Marbois's home. He told Monroe that he was going, but as Monroe had not yet presented his credentials to the French government it did not seem proper for him to go along. The effect of this situation upon the new arrival's already injured dignity can be imagined.

Marbois and Livingston had a lengthy discussion, and finally Marbois told of the conversation he had had with Napoleon two days previously in which the first consul had said that he was determined to sell Louisiana in order to get money for the impending war with England. According to Marbois, Napoleon had told him, "Well, you have charge of the Treasury; let them give you one hundred million francs . . . and take the whole country."

Livingston by his expression showed his surprise at the amount demanded. Marbois assured him that he himself also thought the price too great, but that was what Napoleon wanted for Louisiana. (In fact, of course, Napoleon had set the price at fifty million, but the crafty Marbois said nothing of that.) He pressed Livingston to make a counter offer sufficiently close to Napoleon's supposed price that Marbois could mention to him. Livingston declined; before going further he would have to consult with Monroe. But the negotiations were now fully begun, and Livingston returned home in a jubilant mood.

The next day was occupied with presenting Monroe to Talleyrand, but on April 15 the two Americans met the minister of

James Monroe, who aided in negotiating the Louisiana Purchase, later became fifth president of the United States.

the treasury again for further negotiations, and offered forty million francs. Barbé-Marbois indicated that he was not interested and the conference broke up; that evening, however, he appeared at a dinner party that Livingston was attending, and Livingston told him that fifty million francs was the highest bid the United States would make.

The Agreement
for the Purchase

Negotiations continued. On April 27 Livingston and Marbois gathered at the lodgings of Monroe, who was ill and lay on a couch during the proceedings.

Marbois opened the conversation by giving the Americans a draft treaty that he said was the one proposed by Napoleon. It asked one hundred million francs and in addition required the United States to pay twenty million francs of claims held against France by United States citizens. The French minister said, however, that he himself felt that was asking too much, and he produced another draft he had prepared that reduced the amount to eighty million francs, including the claims.

Polite haggling followed at much length. Livingston and Marbois argued about whether or not the claims of United States citizens should be considered a part of the negotiations for Louisiana or should be handled separately. Marbois and Monroe also argued about provisions that would give France special commercial privileges in the territory after it became the property of the United States. And Livingston gave Marbois a lengthy document that contained some American "observations" on the subject of Louisiana, which the minister promised that he would show to Napoleon.

On the 29th the two Americans called upon Marbois and gave him a written counterproposal: the United States would pay fifty million francs and assume the twenty millions in claims, a total of seventy million francs, in return for Louisiana. Marbois replied that he could not continue negotiations unless the United States offered at least eighty millions in all; Napoleon would accept nothing less.

[21]

Livingston and Monroe knew that Napoleon was changeable, and that should he become displeased he would be fully capable of deciding not to sell Louisiana at all. If they had also known the pressures that Napoleon's brothers were putting upon him to keep the territory, they might even have hesitated to bargain as far as they had. Upon receiving this flat statement from Marbois, the Americans agreed to the eighty million francs, the equivalent of fifteen million dollars.

In the discussion that followed, the treasury minister pressed for some part of the payment to be made immediately while the Americans held out for all payments to be over a longer period. Marbois agreed to drop most of the requirements for French commercial privileges. Yet he did raise Napoleon's point that the inhabitants of Louisiana must have the rights of United States citizens, and the American representatives agreed to incorporate it. They then left the whole matter in the hands of Marbois, who was to see Napoleon for final approval the next day.

On Sunday, May 1, at the palace of the Louvre, Monroe was officially presented to Napoleon by Livingston. Afterward they dined with the first consul, and following the meal there was polite conversation about the new city of Washington, which was then nearing completion, and about President Jefferson. But there was no mention of Louisiana. By 8:30 that evening, however, the two American ministers were again closeted with Marbois at his house, and another long discussion of the proposed treaty was under way.

The French and American representatives went over the draft one point at a time, making whatever changes seemed necessary. For example, as Monroe noted, "The articles at the close of our project which respected the cession and transfer of the territory, he proposed to put together in the commencement, which we examined and modified somewhat by consent."

Official signing of the purchase agreement in the Louvre early in May 1803, is depicted in this painting. Actual document bore the date of April 30. Napoleon, center, shakes hands with the Americans.

On May 2, 1803, the three men signed the documents —
which bore the date of April 30 — making the agreement official.
As soon as they had signed, the three rose and shook hands joy-
fully, knowing that they had participated in an historic act — an
act that several later historians would call the greatest diplomatic
achievement of the United States. "We have lived long," said
Livingston, "but this is the noblest work of our whole lives."

Ratification
and Debate

When President Jefferson learned, early in July, that his ministers had bought not just New Orleans but all Louisiana he was faced with a dream come true. But he was also troubled by a matter of principle. He had always insisted on such a strict interpretation of the Constitution that he could do nothing that was not officially authorized in it; and the Constitution did not expressly give the president the right to buy territories. Throughout the summer, Jefferson wrestled with his conscience and consulted his advisors. Should he not ask for an amendment of the Constitution to permit him to do what in effect he already had done? Finally the president decided that for the good of the nation he should adopt a broad construction of his power under the Constitution, assume that the action was legal, and forget the idea of an amendment.

In his Third Annual Message to Congress, on October 17, Jefferson announced the transfer of Louisiana from France to the United States and said that when the transfer had been ratified by the Senate the matter would be laid before the House "for the exercise of their functions," that is, primarily, to provide the necessary money. Three days later, the treaty was formally ratified by the Senate, although the Federalists, the opposition party, objected violently.

The Federalists had always favored just such a broad construction of the Constitution as Jefferson now put forth and had opposed his previous philosophy of narrow construction. But the Federalists were basically a party of the mercantile northeastern states. They feared that the huge new territory would become mainly agricultural and that by joining their agrarian rivals of the

South and West would outnumber them. So they fought to keep Louisiana from becoming part of the Union.

After ratification, Congress had to provide the funds and make the other arrangements for taking over Louisiana. The debates that accompanied this action in both chambers, however, had more to do with the legality of the treaty than with the matters at hand. They were debates that more logically might have preceded ratification and that could now have little effect. However they did show the feelings of the various parties and in the end they strengthened the power of the national government.

In the House of Representatives, Gaylord Griswold of New York proposed a resolution asking that the president lay the treaty and related documents before the House to show whether or not the United States really had acquired title to Louisiana. The opposition to this motion was led by John Randolph of Virginia. The motion then was trimmed down to ask only for the treaty and some specific evidence that Spain had transferred the territory to France, but it still failed to pass by a narrow margin, 57 votes for to 59 against.

The following day the House considered a motion for putting the treaty into effect. But Gaylord Griswold argued that the treaty was unconstitutional. He based this contention on two points. First, he said, the treaty-making power did not extend to adding foreign people and territory to the United States — people and territory that "might overbalance the existing territory, and thereby the rights of the present citizens of the United States . . . be swallowed up and lost." Second, the treaty gave French and Spanish ships special privileges for twelve years in the port of New Orleans — although the Constitution provided that "no preference shall be given by any regulation of commerce to ports of one State over another."

In answer to this, the Jeffersonian Republicans (the political

[26]

ancestors of today's Democrats) argued that the Constitution could not restrict the country to particular limits, and that in fact the power of the Constitution to revise limits and settle disputes had already been frequently used. If this power existed in the government, it necessarily had to be held by the president, who was responsible for dealing with foreign governments. So far as the constitutional ban on preferential treatment to the ports of one state was concerned, Louisiana was not a state at all, but a territory that had been purchased by the United States. And, said John Randolph, "I regard this stipulation as a part of the price of the territory. It was a condition which the party ceding had a right to require, and to which we had a right to assent."

When the matter came to a vote, the carrying out of the treaty was approved by 90 to 25. Of the 25 congressmen voting against it, all were Federalists and 17 were from New England.

Soon afterward the Senate considered the same matter. Again, each side paraded the same arguments. Timothy Pickering of Massachusetts stated the basic Federalist position: "I believe the assent of each individual state to be necessary for the admission of a foreign country as an associate in the Union, in like manner as in a commercial house the consent of each member would be necessary to admit a new partner into the company."

Later in the Senate debate, Uriah Tracy of Connecticut put the Federalist argument most concisely: "The relative strength which this admission gives to a Southern and Western interest is contradictory to the principles of our original Union." The crux of the matter was fear by the northeastern states that they would be outnumbered. Tracy went on to say:

I have no doubt but we can obtain territory either by conquest or compact, even all Louisiana and a thousand times more if you please, without violating the Constitution. We can hold territory; but to admit the inhabitants into the Union, to make citizens of them, and States, by treaty, we cannot constitutionally do. . . . If done at all, they must be done by universal consent of all the States . . . and this universal consent I am positive can never be obtained by such a pernicious measure as the admission of Louisiana. . . . This would be absorbing the Northern states, and rendering them as insignificant in the Union as they ought to be, if by their own consent the measure should be adopted.

But when the vote was taken in the Senate, the measure passed by 26 to 5. There was now no question that the Louisiana Purchase — as the vast new territory was to be known — belonged to the United States. Even though the Federalists wanted to rule the new territory as though it were a colony and their opponents wanted to bring it into the Union, every speaker, regardless of party and regardless of other differences, agreed that the United States government could acquire new land by conquest or purchase. As the historian Henry Adams said, "For the first time in the national history all parties agreed in admitting that the government could govern."

The Organization of
the Louisiana Purchase

The next matter to come before Congress was the way in which the Louisiana Purchase was to be governed. In the discussion that followed, party lines were not followed as strictly as in the earlier debate. The main argument centered on a particular provision of the bill:

> *That, until Congress shall have made provisions for the temporary government of the said Territories, all the military, civil, and judicial powers, exercised by the officers of the existing government of the same, shall be vested in such person and persons, and shall be exercised in such manner, as the President of the United States shall direct.*

For a number of legislators of the day, this gave the president altogether too much authority, and even men of Jefferson's own party such as John Randolph offered amendments designed to trim away or limit presidential authority within the purchase before Congress provided for its government. On the other hand, some New England legislators supported the measure simply on practical grounds. How better or more simply could the situation be handled? To be sure, some of the more extreme speakers declared that Jefferson was now stepping into the place of the king of Spain, who had recently ceded the territory, and was himself becoming a despot on American soil. Nevertheless the bill passed easily and was approved by the president on October 31.

This bill was a temporary measure that was necessary for the United States to take possession of the Louisiana Purchase. Since more permanent arrangements had to follow, a Senate committee headed by John Breckenridge of Kentucky set out to draft a bill by which the purchase would be governed and administered. The Breckenridge Bill, as it finally passed, divided the purchase into two parts. The more heavily populated southern part (essentially the present-day state of Louisiana) was to become the Territory of Orleans; the sparsely inhabited but much larger northern part was to be the District of Louisiana. The Territory of Orleans would have a governor, secretary, legislative council, and judges appointed by the president — provisions similar to those operative in other territories that had not yet become states. The District of Louisiana would come under the government of the Territory of Indiana.

Transfer of
the Louisiana Puchase

President Jefferson appointed William E. C. Claiborne, governor of Mississippi Territory, and General James Wilkinson, Commander-in-Chief of the United States Army, as commissioners to receive the Louisiana Purchase in the name of the United States. The transfer from France to the United States took place in the city of New Orleans on December 20, 1803, less than a month after the formal transfer of the territory from Spain to France. Pierre Clement de Laussat, the recently arrived French governor, acted for Napoleon.

On the morning prior to the ceremony the provincial militia assembled in the Place d'Armes of the city. Shortly before noon, a signal gun announced that the American delegation had left its camp and was approaching; another gun announced when they passed a halfway mark. Then the French batteries (which were still manned by Spanish artillerymen) fired a twenty-four-gun salute. At twelve o'clock, the Americans marched into the Place d'Armes, escorted by a company of grenadiers from the city militia who had met them at the gate. At their head rode Claiborne and Wilkinson; behind the commissioners came American dragoons, artillery, and infantry. The American troops, drums beating, formed on the river side of the square opposite the French troops, and the two commissioners dismounted and proceeded up the steps to the large council hall within the City Hall building.

After Claiborne and Wilkinson had been received by high officials and important citizens, they were escorted to seats on a balcony overlooking the square. In his account of the events Laussat recorded that the other eleven balconies of the City Hall

were filled with beautiful women. All around the square, well-dressed people sat in their balconies to witness the ceremony.

Laussat sat in the middle; the two commissioners sat on lower chairs on either side of him. The French governor opened the ceremony and then had lesser officials read the treaty aloud in both French and English. Following that he read his own credentials and his orders authorizing him to transfer the colony. Claiborne read his orders to receive it. Laussat handed the keys of the city to Claiborne, ushered him to the highest seat, and then sat down in the chair that Claiborne had vacated.

Claiborne followed with a speech in English congratulating the people "on an event so advantageous to yourselves, and so glorious to united America." Then the official documents of transfer were read in French and English, and exchanged between the commissioners. Finally, the French Tricolor was slowly lowered from the flagpole at the same time that the Stars and Stripes was hoisted. There was a brief pause at the halfway point when the two flags were at the same level; a signal cannon was fired; then amidst cannon salutes and musketry, the American flag rose to the top of the staff.

Finally, a French sergeant-major gathered in the old flag, wrapped it around his body, and marched with drawn sword to the center of the militia. There Laussat joined them, and the company marched off with drums beating. The United States troops presented arms as they passed.

New Orleans, December 1803. Stars and stripes are hoisted as the French tricolor is hauled down, signifying the official transfer of Louisiana from France to the United States.

[33]

The Role of
James Wilkinson

General James Wilkinson, the man who helped to accept Louisiana for the United States, had had a long history of service to his country, and although it was not generally known, an equally long history of treachery. Wilkinson had settled in the frontier district of Kentucky — a district separated from most of the United States by mountains and dependent largely upon the Ohio and Mississippi rivers for transportation of heavy cargoes. In 1787 he sent by boat to New Orleans a sizable quantity of tobacco, flour, and bacon. He followed his goods down to the Spanish colony determined, as he later put it in a letter to one of the Spanish officials, to seek the "patronage" of Spain.

Once in New Orleans Wilkinson went to the Spanish governor and suggested that Kentucky could well be separated from the United States and brought under the rule of Spain. He would be happy, he said, to bring this about if the Spanish government would grant him a yearly pension in return. Before he left New Orleans on that mission, he signed an agreement that the governor promptly sent off to the Spanish court at Madrid. Thereafter Wilkinson received from Spain regular payments of the then-impressive sum of $2,000 per year. In fact, these payments continued after President Washington commissioned him a colonel in the United States Army and he became one of the key officers on the western frontier. While Wilkinson was unable to separate Kentucky from the rest of the country, he undoubtedly did many smaller favors for his Spanish masters. In due course he was made

A portrait of General James Wilkinson by St. Memin.

[34]

a brigadier general in the United States Army and in 1795 he became its Commander-in-Chief.

Now, on that December day in 1803, as Wilkinson sat looking over the Place d'Armes of New Orleans and graciously acting out his part in accepting Louisiana, his personal interests were not far from his mind. When the ceremony was over, he retired from the public view and quietly sought out the Spanish officials who still remained in the city. Spain, he reminded them, had not paid him his pension for some years and was $20,000 behind; now he wanted that amount. After some dickering, Wilkinson agreed to a smaller cash settlement and also agreed that he would continue to submit information. Later he wrote a report that among other things advised the Spaniards to arrest the members of the Lewis and Clark Expedition, who were just setting out in their first exploration of the Louisiana Purchase.

Lewis and Clark
Start Out

During the winter of 1803-04, the expedition that President Jefferson had long dreamed of camped on the eastern side of the Mississippi River, near the mouth of the Missouri, waiting for spring and the start of their journey. Captain Lewis had selected as his joint commander William Clark, with whom he had previously served in the army. Clark, the youngest brother of George Rogers Clark, had several years before resigned his commission as a regular army officer, but he gladly joined Lewis in this adventure and was reappointed in the army. Both officers had had experience with wilderness life and both had held commands. In 1803 Lewis was 29 years old and Clark was 33.

To quote Bernard DeVoto, a leading historian of American westward expansion, "Both were men of great intelligence, of distinguished intelligence. The entire history of North American exploration contains no one who could be called their intellectual equal." The two men worked together in a way few human beings ever do; they were absolutely equal in command and they seem always to have agreed with each other. They selected the men of their expedition carefully, and during their winter wait they trained them and hardened them physically.

In addition to its two leaders, the expedition was made up of nine Kentucky frontiersmen, fourteen soldiers all of whom were volunteers, two French voyageurs, an interpreter and hunter, and a black slave named York who belonged to Clark. All these men except York were enlisted in the army and three of them were appointed sergeants. There were also an additional corporal, six privates, and nine voyageurs who were to assist the others until they reached their winter camp and were then to return. On May

14, 1804, they set out under command of Clark in a large keelboat fifty-five feet long and in two smaller open boats; two horses were led along the river bank to provide transportation for hunting and exploration.

Lewis, who had been making his last official visit to the headquarters at St. Louis, arrived and joined them on the 20th. The party then moved steadily along the Missouri. Usually Clark was in charge of the boats while Lewis explored the shore, hunting and making notes on the terrain and the wildlife.

By the middle of June the weather was hot. Clark noted in his journal on the 17th, with his unique spelling and usage

The party is much afflicted with Boils, and Several have the Deassentary, which I contribute to the water. The Countrey about this place is butifull in the river rich and well timbered on the S.S. [starboard side]. . . . On the L.S. [larboard side] the high lands & Prairie coms in the bank of the river and continus back, well watered and abounds in Deer Elk & Bear. The Ticks & Musquiters are very troublesome.

On they went, rowing the heavy boats past snags, through sudden storms, and against fast currents. The water was so muddy that it was impossible to see any obstacles below the surface, whether they were sandbars, snags, or rocks. At times the boats had to be towed by the men trudging along the banks, hauling on lines.

Game of all sorts was plentiful; Lewis later wrote to his mother, "our prospect for starving is therefore consequently small." Early in August the expedition met a small band of Oto and Mis-

The Charles Willson Peale portrait of William Clark, who, with Meriwether Lewis, led the famous expedition westward to explore the Louisiana territory.

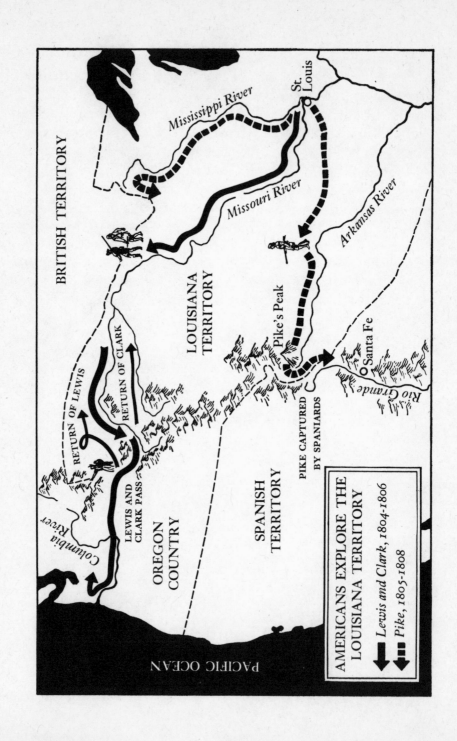

AMERICANS EXPLORE THE LOUISIANA TERRITORY

souri Indians which contained several chiefs of secondary rank. This was the first of many such groups they would encounter. The leaders of the expedition and the Indians held a council in which the white men expressed their friendship and presented gifts to the Indians, and the latter made polite speeches of welcome.

By the end of October they had reached a place in what today is central North Dakota, in the country of the Mandan Indians. The Mandans had several villages, each surrounded by mud walls and ditches to protect them against wandering Sioux war parties. With them lived a few Frenchmen. As the weather was becoming cold, Lewis and Clark decided to build a fortification nearby and spend the winter there. The expedition raised a structure of cottonwood logs on the river a little distance below the Indian villages; this work was called Fort Mandan.

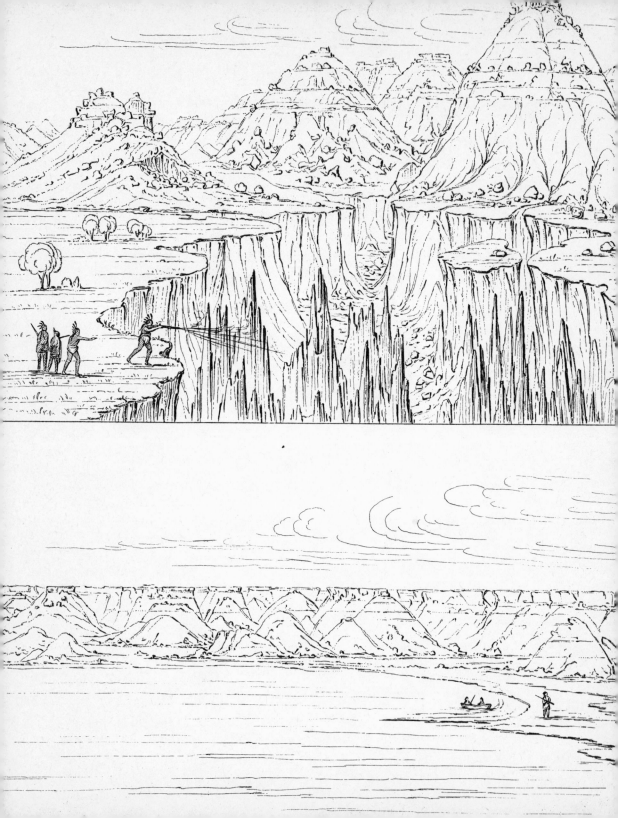

Lewis and Clark
Turn West

Throughout the winter they obtained information not only from the Mandans and other visiting Indians, but particularly from the nearby Minnetarees who traveled widely. They learned about the Plains tribes and about the geography of the West, preparing lengthy reports that were sent back to Jefferson when the keelboat returned in the spring and that Jefferson in turn presented to Congress. They also sent the president a vast collection of animal skins, a few small live animals, and some Indian artifacts. During the winter they made contact with representatives of some Canadian fur companies; they were reasonably friendly, announcing that the United States now owned the territory but that the Canadians might still trade there, subject, however, to American competition.

York, Clark's black servant, was a giant whose strength was a marvel to the Indians. So were his skin and his hair; Indians, whenever they first saw him, crowded around to admire. The Indian children crowded around too, until they became a nuisance and York would roar at them, making himself "more turribel than we wished," according to Clark.

During the winter a French trader, Touissant Charbonneau, who had worked for some of the British fur companies, appeared at Fort Mandan. He said he wanted to join the expedition as interpreter. Since he could speak the language of the Minnetarees, which white men found particularly difficult, he was hired to accompany the group.

Scenes from Mandan Indian country in North Dakota, as drawn by the frontier artist George Catlin.

On March 25, 1805, Clark noted in his journal, "Saw Swans & Wild Gees flying N.E. this evening." It was time, too, for the expedition to be moving. On April 7 they sent the keelboat on its way back to St. Louis, with the corporal in charge, five soldiers, and some of the voyageurs. The remainder of the group set out upriver in six dugout canoes they had made, plus the two smaller boats they had brought with them. At that point, the Missouri River comes almost directly from the west; as a result they now were traveling west, rather than north and a bit west as they had done most of the way from St. Louis.

Lewis, Clark, their two interpreters, and the young Indian wife of Charbonneau who carried her infant of less than two months, all shared a "tent of dressed skins" — a tepee. The Indian woman, actually a girl of about seventeen, whom most of the men of the expedition called "Janey," had the Indian name of Saca-jawea. She was a member of the Snake nation, which lived on the far side of the Rockies, and had been captured by a Minnetaree raid-ing party from whom her husband had later bought her. She quickly proved her usefulness by finding edible roots, explaining the strange plants and animals they found, sewing buckskin cloth-ing, and interpreting the occasional old signs of passing Indian bands that they saw.

By April 25, Lewis, working along the shore in advance of the main body which had been slowed by cold and windy weather, reached the mouth of the Yellowstone River. He noted in his journal, "the whole face of the country was covered with herds of Buffalo, Elk & Antelopes; deer are also abundant, but keep themselves more concealed in the woodland. The buffaloe Elk and Antelope are so gentle that we pass near them while feed-ing, without appearing to excite any alarm among them; and when we attract their attention, they frequently approach us more nearly

[44]

to discover what we are, and in some instances pursue us a considerable distance apparently with that view."

On the 28th they moved on again; next day, walking along the shore, Lewis and one of his men encountered their first two grizzly bears and killed one of them. Although other travelers had mentioned grizzlies, Lewis was able to write the first detailed description of one.

The explorers found their way by a combination of celestial navigation and directions they had gathered from the Indians. By June 3 the party reached the juncture of two large rivers, one of which according to Indian instructions would take them near the headwaters of the Columbia River. After preliminary explorations they decided that the southern fork must be the right one. Lewis and four men set out on foot along the southern fork to see if they could find the falls of the Missouri that the Indians had told them about. If the falls turned out to be on the southern branch then that must be the main river. The remainder of the party busied themselves digging cellars in which to store part of the provisions and in preparing one of the boats that was to be left behind. Sacajawea was "verry" sick and Clark, following the medical theories of the day, bled her.

On June 13 Lewis was proceeding along the river when his "ears were saluted with the agreeable sound of a fall of water." Then he saw spray rising over the plain like a cloud of smoke; it disappeared in the wind and rose again; he had reached the falls. There were five of them in a ten-mile stretch, the tallest being the farthest upstream; Lewis called it the Great Falls. He returned to the base camp on the 16th with the happy news, but was disconcerted to find Sacajawea so ill. "This gave me some concern as well for the poor object herself, then with a young child in her arms, as from the consideration of her being our only dependence for a

friendly negociation with the Snake Indians on whom we must depend for horses to assist in our portage from the Mississippi to the Columbia River."

Lewis took over the task of doctoring her while Clark and five men set out to inspect the falls and decide upon the portages they would use to get around them. Lewis gave to Sacajawea some of the medicines — "barks and opium" — that they had, plus some water from a sulfur spring. Her sickness, he concluded, "originated principally from an obstruction of the mensis in concequence of taking could." The next day she was free of pain and clear of fever and ate as much as Lewis would let her.

Meanwhile, the men were building wooden wheels and axles to carry the boats and luggage around the falls. On the 20th the main party moved up to a camp at the Great Falls, and for nearly a month thereafter they dragged their boats and gear around the series of falls and rapids. The portage was about eighteen miles long and the ground was covered with cactus; by this time the expedition had only rawhide moccasins to wear, and although they sewed a double layer of hide on the soles, their feet were still stabbed raw. According to Clark, "the men has to haul with all their strength wate & art, maney times every man all catching the grass . . . & stones with their hands to give them more force in drawing on the Canoes & Loads, and notwithstanding the coolness of the air in high perspiration and every halt, those not employed in repairing the course, are asleep in a moment. . . ."

There were sudden storms that carved channels across the portage and turned the clay underfoot to glue. Some of the storms

Above: Captains Lewis and Clark holding a council with the Indians. Below: Captain Clark and his men shooting bears. Both pictures are from the Gass Journal.

consisted of hail, at one time with stones that were "7 inches in circumference & waied 3 ounces," and the men had to take shelter from them. They had heard from the Indians that the country ahead contained little game, so hunting parties were also kept busy building up a supply of dried meat and of rawhide from which all their clothing now was made.

Captain Lewis views the falls of the Missouri. Drawing by J. N. Marchand.

Across the
Continental Divide

Once above the Great Falls they loaded everything into eight dugouts, and on July 15 they set out again. This was mountainous country and there were many small rapids in the river that forced the party to pole their canoes upstream. On the 25th they reached a place where the Missouri split into three forks. The northern fork, which Lewis and Clark named the Jefferson River, contained the most water and seemed to lead more directly toward the west than the others. This is the place where the Missouri River begins, nearly 2,500 miles from its mouth. Lewis, who was in command of the flotilla at the time, halted and made camp, awaiting the return of Clark, who had circled inland on foot, looking for some sign of the Snake Indians from whom they hoped to get horses.

Clark returned to camp without seeing any Indians, but extremely sick, with a high fever that had begun the night before and that was causing him chills and aching muscles. Lewis wrote, "I prevailed on him to take a doze of Rushes pills, which I have always found sovereign in such cases and to bathe his feet in warm water and rest himself." Rushes pills were potent things, each consisting of ten grains of calomel and ten grains of jalap. The party remained there until the 30th. Lewis noted that this was the place where the Minnetaree raiding party had captured Sacajawea.

When Clark felt better and Lewis had made all the scientific observations that he wished in the area, they started up the Jefferson fork. On its way, the party had had frequent encounters with cactus; as a result, several of the men were lame and one of Clark's torn feet became infected.

On August 8, according to Lewis, "the Indian woman recognized the point of a high plain to our right which she informed us was not very distant from the summer retreat of her nation on a river beyond the mountains which runs to the west. . . . She assures us that we shall either find her people on this river or on the river immediately west of its source." They were at the Bitterroot Mountains, which there form the continental divide. Lewis decided that he would take a small party and strike out in search of the headwaters of the westerly-flowing river, and particularly in search of Snake Indians, leaving the rest of the expedition to proceed laboriously upstream.

On the 10th, he found old tracks of horses, but lost them again. On the 11th, he saw a distant horseman, but the Indian quickly disappeared. Following an Indian trail on the 12th, Lewis reached both the ultimate waters of the Missouri, the pass today called Lemhi Pass, and his first stream flowing westward. It now is called the Lemhi River. It was "a handsome bold running Creek of cold Clear water" from which he took a drink. The following day, as they descended into the valley on the far side, they saw two women, a man, and some dogs on a hill some distance ahead, but all of them had vanished by the time the party reached that place.

Shortly afterward they came upon three other women. One of them immediately ran, but an elderly woman and a thirteen-year-old girl were left behind, obviously expecting that the strangers would kill them. By treating these two kindly and giving them some beads and other trade goods, Lewis won their trust; the older woman then called back the young woman who had fled, and she too received her trinkets. Then Lewis painted the cheeks of each of them with vermilion, a sign of peace among the Indians, and by further signs asked them to take him to their camp.

Some two miles farther on, the expedition was met by about sixty warriors who came toward them quickly on horseback. Lewis, leaving his gun behind, advanced about fifty paces toward them. The leader of the warriors also advanced a little and spoke to the women, who explained what had happened and showed the presents they had received. "These men," wrote Lewis, "then advanced and embraced me very affectionately in their way which is by puting their left arm over your right shoulder clasping your back, while they apply their left cheek to yours and frequently vociferate the word *ah-hi-e, a-hi-e,* that is, I am much pleased, I am much rejoiced." Lewis continued: "Both parties now advanced and we wer all carresed and besmeared with their grease and paint til I was heartily tired of the national hug."

On the 15th, Lewis started back toward the river, accompanied by a chief and a number of other Indians. As they went on, a number of Indians left them; upon arriving at the river and discovering that Clark and the main body had not yet reached that point, many of the remainder became suspicious. Lewis realized that if they decided to abandon him they would spread the alarm among any other bands in the neighborhood, and he would not be able to make further contact with any of them. Thus he would not be able to get any horses.

But next morning it developed that the rest of the expedition was only a short way downstream. Clark, Charbonneau, and his wife Sacajawea were walking along the shore when the Indian girl began to dance with excitement; she turned to Clark and pointed out several Indians who were approaching on horseback. She told him that they were people from her own tribe. Among the approaching group was one of Lewis's party, with a message from Lewis explaining what had happened. Clark and his two companions then went ahead with the Indians to meet Lewis and the group with him. There Sacajawea was embraced by another

A map drawn by Captain Clark of a portion of the Missouri River with indications of camps on the outward and homeward tour.

N. 85 W. 2 to a point of ...
the river making ...
to North ...
S. W. ... along the bend ...
S. W. ... to a point of woodland ...
shaping a small island a
mile in length commencing
at one mile opposite ...
the lower point of ...
encamped on the head ...
... below

21

the 17th of May 1805

Brush Lodge Creek

Campd the 16th of May 1805

Campd this 18th

Course & Distance 19th May 1805

S. 85° W. 1¾ to a point of woodland on the
Larboard opposite to a bluff S.S.

N. ... 1½ to a point of timber on the Starboard
opposite a bluff & high hills on L.S.

N. W. 1 mile to a point of woodland Lard side
opposite to a bluff

N. E. 1½ to a willow point Star. the river
making a deep bend to the E.

N. ... 1 along the Star. side opposite to a bluff

N. W. 2½ to a point of woodland Lard. side opposite
to a bluff

... ¾ along the Lard. shore opposite a ...

S. W. ½ along the Lard. point opposite to a bluff

S. W. 3 to a point of woodland Star. opposite
a bluff the river making a bend to South

N. W. 1½ to a point on Lard. side low ...

N. W. ¾ to the point of high land on the Lard. ...

N. W. 1¾ to a point of willow or Star. opposite a bluff

... 1 ... to a point of low bottom on the Lard point ...
lower ... of a ... island in the bend ...

woman who recognized her, while Clark was introduced both to the chief and to the embraces of the Snake nation.

A council followed in a circular shelter of willows that the Indians had built. After the initial ceremonies, one of the Americans sent for Sacajawea to act as interpreter. She came in, sat down, and began to interpret. Then suddenly she recognized that the chief was her brother, ran to him, embraced him, weeping, and threw her blanket over him.

After this emotional reunion the council proceeded. Lewis and Clark arranged to buy horses from the Indians and tried to convince them of the benefits they would gain now that the United States owned this territory. During the remainder of the month, the expedition explored the rivers on the western side of the continental divide, trying unsuccessfully to find one that was navigable. They sank the dugouts in a pond near the headwaters of the Missouri where they could be found and raised again, and generally prepared to continue their journey. Then they moved their base camp to the Indian village that Lewis had found, and were helped in their various efforts by the Indians.

Late in August, the expedition moved on toward the Pacific. After hardships at least as great as those already encountered, they succeeded in reaching the Pacific Coast in mid-October. After considerable local exploration, they decided on a site for their winter fort, which they named Fort Clatsop, after a local Indian tribe.

Political Disaffection

Meantime, back in the United States, the Federalists were greatly disturbed at the end of 1803 and the beginning of 1804 by the following events. John Pickering, a district judge of New Hampshire was impeached; and the impeachment of Samuel Chase, a Supreme Court justice, was threatened. Both men were ardently supported by the Federalists. There were moves to adopt the Twelfth Amendment, which required separate ballots for president and vice president. (Previously the man with the most votes became president and the man with the second most became vice president.) And, finally, there was the inclusion of the Louisiana Purchase within the United States. All these developments tended to move power away from the northern states and to give it either to the nation as a whole or to the national government and the party in power; of them all, however, the introduction of Louisiana into the Union seemed most clearly against the interests of the North.

Somehow New England had to protect herself, or so thought many of the New England Federalists. Actually, a majority of New England Federalist Senators felt it was inevitable that the northeast would in time secede from the Union; but in January of 1804 an influential group of New Englanders began a movement toward more immediate secession. Roger Griswold, the congressman from Connecticut who had strongly opposed the Louisiana treaty, wrote on March 11

> *The project which we had formed was to induce, if possible, the legislatures of the three New England States who remain Federal [i.e., which the Federalists controlled] to commence measures which should call for a reunion of the Northern*

States. . . . The magnitude and jealousy of Massachusetts would render it necessary that the operation should be commenced there. If any hope can be created that New York will ultimately support the plan, it may perhaps be supported.

Other Federalists sympathized, but advised a more moderate course. One of them, George Cabot, wrote, "A separation at some period not very remote may probably take place. . . . If we should be made to feel a very great calamity from the abuse of power by the National Administration, we might do almost anything. . . . [But] a separation now is impracticable, because we do not feel the necessity or utility of it."

The more extreme Federalists were not to be dissuaded, however. Among the leaders of the secessionist group was Timothy Pickering, the Massachusetts Senator who during the Louisiana debate had compared the states of the Union with partners in a business firm. He was determined that in order to help his movement New York must be brought into the Federalist camp; and to accomplish this he needed a New Yorker who would be willing to join him. There was one logical man who might lend himself to such a project — none other than the vice president of the United States, who was then nearing the end of his term, Aaron Burr.

General Wilkinson had meanwhile become friendly with Burr. As Bernard DeVoto wrote, "the orbits of our most tireless small scoundrel and our scoundrel of genius had now reached conjunction." These two were able to put the purchase of Louisiana to their own advantage. The District of Louisiana was about to be made the Territory of Louisiana, a political division that required several administrative officers, and Burr persuaded Jefferson to appoint Wilkinson as governor and Burr's brother-in-law, Dr. Joseph Browne, as territorial secretary.

[56]

Jefferson and Burr were on strained terms, however, and Burr was less successful in his request for some political appointment for himself after his term as vice president expired; Jefferson politely turned him down. Soon afterward, Burr fell in with Pickering's plan and decided to run for the governorship of New York, with the backing of the extreme Federalists. (It is not known whether he agreed with their secessionist aims, but it is evident that he would make almost any move to advance his own interests.) Burr's candidacy would automatically have brought him into conflict with the moderate New York Federalist leader, Alexander Hamilton, even if the two men had not already disliked each other.

Burr won the nomination, but this only doubled Hamilton's determination to oppose him; throughout the campaign Hamilton and Burr struggled behind the scenes. Burr lost the election and the secessionist movement soon collapsed. The extent to which Hamilton contributed to that defeat is uncertain, but in Burr's mind he was fully responsible for it. Two months afterward, Aaron Burr sent to Alexander Hamilton some newspaper clippings that dated from the election campaign and that quoted Hamilton as calling Burr "despicable"; with them he sent a letter asking Hamilton to affirm or deny that he had made the statement. Hamilton answered politely enough, but ended, "I trust on more reflection you will see the matter in the same light with me; if not, I can only regret the circumstances and must abide the consequences." It was the usual form for accepting a challenge to a duel.

Aaron Burr

On July 11, 1804, Aaron Burr shot Alexander Hamilton and Hamilton died on the afternoon of the following day. On July 27 Burr left his New York home for Philadelphia. A New York coroner's jury found that he had murdered Hamilton and a New York jury indicted him for sending a challenge. Although the duel had taken place in New Jersey and New York had no jurisdiction over the act itself, Burr nevertheless went to Georgia to escape possible extradition. Later in the year, he returned to Washington for the new session of Congress at about the time a New Jersey grand jury indicted him for murder. On February 13, 1805, he presided over the counting of the electoral votes that reelected Jefferson and that elected George Clinton vice president. On March 2, Burr made a short farewell address to the Senate, moving it to tears, and walked out, leaving behind him the ruins of his political career.

That same month Burr was in touch with a minister of the British government, suggesting that Britain might provide half a million dollars and a fleet in the Gulf of Mexico to help separate the Louisiana Purchase from the United States and make it an independent country. The British response was unenthusiastic. The idea of turning the purchase into his own personal empire, however, seems to have remained with Burr. In April he crossed the mountains to Pittsburgh on horseback; there he was to meet Wilkinson, but the general did not arrive in time. Burr wrote to him, asking to meet him at Louisville, adding, "I have some things to say which cannot be written." Early in May, Burr and two friends, Mr. and Mrs. Gabriel Shaw, set out down the Ohio on a

A portrait of Aaron Burr.

boat that was typical of river transport of that day. He described it in a letter to his daughter: "Properly speaking a floating house, sixty feet by fourteen, containing diningroom, kitchen with fireplace, and two bedrooms; roofed from stem to stern; steps to go up, and a walk on top the whole length; glass windows, &c."

Burr paused at Cincinnati, where he had lengthy discussions with some friends; after he left, rumors began to fly that the western part of the United States was going to separate from the Union. At Louisville he left his boat, going inland on horseback to Frankfort and Lexington, then southward to Nashville. At each city he was closeted with friends. Near Nashville he stayed for four days at the Hermitage, Andrew Jackson's home. There he informed Jackson that Henry Dearborn, Jefferson's secretary of war, was secretely working with him to separate the West. His host provided an open boat, which took him down the Cumberland to Fort Massic, a post on the Ohio River, and there he finally joined Wilkinson.

During their meeting, the general gave Burr letters of introduction to important people in New Orleans. He then provided the former vice president with a barge, rowed by ten men and commanded by a sergeant, and in this conveyance Burr continued downriver, stopping for a time at Natchez and reaching New Orleans on June 26.

The Burr–
Wilkinson Plot

There was at that time a strong feeling among some Americans in recently acquired New Orleans that the United States should go farther and take over Mexico, and one of the local newspapers had called for an army of "liberation" to seize the area from Spain. Burr engaged in a round of social and other activity in the city, making contact with many of the important inhabitants, some of whom agreed to help him foment a Mexican revolution. After some time spent in such planning, Burr returned to St. Louis by horseback, again visiting a number of friends en route.

St. Louis was the headquarters of General Wilkinson. He and Burr spent several days together; Burr later told Andrew Jackson that the two of them had completed their plan for an attack on Mexico during that time. But simultaneously, Wilkinson was having a steady correspondence with the Spaniards, making plans that the Louisiana Purchase, and if possible other western areas, would break away from the United States.

Burr left St. Louis and started toward Nashville. On August 2 the *United States Gazette*, a Philadelphia newspaper, published an article that asked if Burr was going to call a convention of the states and territories bordering on the Ohio and Mississippi rivers. The convention's purpose would be to form a separate government and then to use the military installations and supplies in the area, especially at New Orleans, to attack Mexico with the aid of the British. What information the editors had is not known, but it was much too close to the truth for the comfort of the conspirators. The article was followed by others in other papers that sounded variations on the theme, and rumors about every variety of revolution began to spread throughout the West. The information also

[61]

seems to have reached the ears of the Spanish government, for in October some six hundred more Spanish soldiers were moved into Pensacola, then still held by Spain.

As it became evident that Burr was less than discreet and that he had talked too much, Wilkinson's friendship for him began to cool. The general now began to look for ways in which he could both divorce himself from Burr's plans and profit by them.

Toward the end of the year, Burr returned to Philadelphia. Throughout the winter he approached various people who might help him. He visited Washington, D.C., and then went to Charleston to see his daughter, who was married to Joseph Alston, a rich South Carolinian who contributed heavily to Burr's cause. In February Burr was back in Washington, where he had an interview with Jefferson and again tried to obtain a government appointment of some kind, in part by making veiled threats of the harm that he might do if he was not placated. Jefferson did not oblige.

Boundary Difficulties

Early in 1806, serious boundary difficulties began to arise between the United States and Spain.

From the beginning, the boundaries of the Louisiana Purchase had been poorly defined. When the American negotiators asked Barbé-Marbois for a definition and he in turn asked Napoleon, the first consul's comment was, "If an obscurity did not exist, it would perhaps be good policy to put one there." Livingston also pressed Talleyrand for a specific definition without result, later writing:

> *He said he did not know; we must take it as they had received it. I asked him how Spain meant to give them possession? He said, according to the words of the treaty. But what did you mean to take? I do not know. Then you mean that we shall construe it our own way? I can give you no direction; you have made a noble bargain for yourselves, and I suppose you will make the most of it.*

When Jefferson submitted to Congress a description of the new territory he said that the northern and western boundaries were obscure. He did not include Texas in the description, though he believed part of it was included; before making any public statement on Texas, he wanted to study the matter further.

After the ceremonies accepting the purchase in December, 1803, however, Claiborne and Wilkinson reported to the president that the French governor, Laussat, had told them the territory definitely extended to the Rio Grande. As a result of this report, Jefferson concluded that the Louisiana Purchase did include all of Texas. A House committee with whom the President had been working, in March 1804 even defined the extent of the purchase as including the lands *beyond* the Rockies, "between the territories claimed by Great Britain on the one side, and by Spain on the other, quite to the South Sea [the Pacific]." By this definition, Oregon was also included in the territory purchased.

Spain, however, was much upset by the sale of Louisiana in direct violation of the French agreement not to sell the territory. It was a move that threatened to bring the United States — whom the Spaniards suspected of wanting to seize their American colonies — directly to their borders. The Spaniards therefore determined to limit the boundaries of the Louisiana Purchase as narrowly as they could.

This boundary problem came to a head in Texas. The Spanish boundary commissioner, the Marqués de Casa Calvo, had arrived in New Orleans early in 1803 and had used the city as a base of operations for nearly two years after the United States controlled it. He reported to Madrid that there would probably be difficulties over the western boundary of the purchase, which both the French and American commissioners believed to lie along the Rio Grande. Casa Calvo, however, advised that Spain must retain as much of Texas as possible.

The Spanish government gathered three thousand settlers to be sent to Texas, but was unable to dispatch most of them because the Napoleonic wars had disrupted shipping. Some settlers and a number of troops did manage to reach the area, however, and a number of Spanish garrisons were established. Toward the end of 1805, Spanish troops established forts in the eastern part of Texas, even east of the Sabine River, the eastern boundary of the region.

Early in 1806, United States troops were ordered to remove one small post, at Adaes on the Red River, and the Spaniards retired from it without incident. But shortly afterward the Spanish governor, Simon Herrera, led six hundred of his soldiers to reinforce the frontier. Colonel T. H. Cushing of the United States Army was then ordered to the region with three companies of soldiers and two field guns.

[64]

Zebulon Pike's Expedition

In the summer of 1806, when Lewis and Clark were making their way back to civilization by much the same northern route they had followed to the Pacific Coast, General Wilkinson organized an expedition to explore the southwestern part of the Louisiana Purchase and to insure the peaceful intentions of the Indians there. To lead it he selected a twenty-six-year-old army lieutenant, Zebulon Pike, who the previous year had effectively taken a similar expedition to the headwaters of the Mississippi. The southwestern effort turned out to be one of the major explorations of the early years of the United States, but also to be one of the most mysterious. Many things about it remain unexplained to this day.

Almost anything set in motion by the crafty Wilkinson deserves careful examination. Evidently Pike's expedition was intended to carry out some hidden purpose for the general, but what that purpose was can only be guessed. Pike himself apparently did not know all about it; Wilkinson even said so in one of his letters. The general sent with Pike a Dr. John Hamilton Robinson, an intelligent and vigorous man of Pike's own age, who was to be surgeon of the party — a rare luxury for a small army detachment and one not even afforded the Lewis and Clark expedition sent out by the president himself. In fact, Robinson himself appears to have been on some special mission for the general. Pike was an efficient officer who could be trusted to get an expedition safely through wild country; Robinson had little experience in the wilderness, but went as messenger or agent for Wilkinson. Both men apparently were necessary to the general's mysterious purpose.

Pike probably did not know of the Burr-Wilkinson plot, but like many young Americans of his day he may have felt that the United States should take over the Spanish colonial holdings in North America. Tensions at that time between the United States and Spain also made it possible that the two nations might go to war. Putting these two things together, Pike was probably not surprised when Wilkinson directed him to go not just to the borders of Louisiana, but all the way to the Spanish colonial capital of Santa Fe, and to note the roads and terrain that he found en route. But the general expressly warned him to avoid any conflict with the Spaniards. Putting it another way, Pike was to escort Robinson to Santa Fe.

Thus Robinson was on some kind of a mission, probably to the Spanish authorities in Mexico. Historians have speculated that it may have been to warn them of the Burr plot against Mexico, or it may have been to work out a settlement of the difficulties between Spain and the United States in Texas. Still another reason for the trip has been suggested. The Spanish colonial authorities were much upset by the sale of the Louisiana Purchase and the thought that Americans would now be pushing out to their frontiers. If a United States Army expedition suddenly appeared on one of those frontiers their incipient panic would increase; and the value to them of General Wilkinson, a spy in a key military position, would also increase. The actual reasons were probably a combination of these things, and there may have been yet other reasons that we do not know.

In any event, Wilkinson also sent word by roundabout means to Don Nemisio Salcedo, the Spanish Captain-General of the Interior Provinces, at his headquarters in Chihuahua, telling him that Pike's expedition was coming. A further interesting point is that Lieutenant James Wilkinson, the general's son, was to be Pike's second-in-command for the first half of the trip; then when the expedition made its final turn westward he was to branch off and work his way back to the Mississippi River.

On July 15, 1806, Pike and his party ("two lieutenants, one surgeon, one sergeant, two corporals, sixteen privates, and one interpreter") left St. Louis in two boats, accompanied by about fifty Osage and Pawnee Indians who were returning to their villages. The expedition pushed out along the Missouri River. One soldier deserted before they were out of settled territory; several others were sick. On the 28th they reached the Osage River and followed it in a southwesterly direction. By August 18 they reached an Osage Indian town. There they left their boats and, after staying for several days with the Indians, they started across the prairies on September 1, carrying their luggage on fifteen pack horses obtained from the Indians. Thirty warriors and one Indian woman accompanied them.

The country contained a great deal of game and the expedition had no difficulty in living off the land. On the 5th they killed a deer, "which was soon roasting before the fire," and on the 6th they found a stream that contained many fish, but they had no net. Pike's journal constantly records their success at hunting. On the 7th they killed four deer; on the 9th an antelope, two deer, and two turkeys; and on the 10th an elk and a deer. On the 12th, the journal says, "Commenced our march at seven o'clock. Passed very rough flint hills. My feet blistered and very sore. I stood on a hill and in one view below me saw buffalo, elk, deer, cabrie [antelope], and panthers." By the 14th, "on the march we were constantly passing through large herds of buffalo, elk, and cabrie, and I have no doubt but one hunter could support 200 men. I prevented the men shooting at the game, not merely because of the scarcity of ammunition but, as I conceived, the laws of morality forbade it also."

On September 25 they reached a Pawnee settlement near the present Kansas–Nebraska boundary. They discovered that the Indians there had recently been given presents of mules, horses, bridles, and blankets by the Spaniards, and they even saw "a very large road on which the Spanish troops returned and on which we

[67]

could yet discover the grass beaten down in the direction which they went." The Spanish force had been sent as a result of Wilkinson's message to the Spanish authorities that Pike was on his way. The Spaniards had arrived too early, had missed him, and had turned back to Santa Fe without him.

Over the next few days, Pike and his men presented gifts to various chiefs at the village, held councils with representatives of the Kans and Osage tribes and smoked pipes of peace with them, and held a grand council with over four hundred Pawnee warriors. On October 7 the expedition started on its way again. Eleven days later it divided. As planned, Lieutenant Wilkinson, with five soldiers and two Osage Indians, went down the Arkansas River in a skin canoe and a dugout that they made on the spot. Wilkinson was to follow the river to the Mississippi. Pike, with the remainder of the party, went up the Arkansas. On October 29 he saw the first wild horses they had encountered. By this time it was snowing and ice was beginning to form on the river. Pike continued to follow the trail of the Spanish cavalry. As he went on into what today is western Kansas he saw great herds of buffalo cows and calves — he estimated that one herd contained 3,000 animals — and of wild horses. The Spanish force that they were following appeared to have been joined by others, so that there were now six to seven hundred men. The trail began to lead into hilly country.

Above: Lieutenant Zebulon Pike, who headed the expedition to explore the southwestern part of the Louisiana Purchase. Below: Pike and his men on the Missouri River.

Pike's Problems

No one really knew how long it took to go from St. Louis to Santa Fe, and both Pike and Wilkinson apparently thought Pike could get there while the weather still was moderate. This was not surprising — after all, Lewis and Clark at first thought they could go from Fort Mandan to the Pacific and back in one summer. Pike and his whole party wore summer clothing; his soldiers did not even have socks. As the weather grew colder, all his group suffered from it.

The weary horses slowed the party and finally two of them gave out and had to be left to fend for themselves. The expedition plodded ahead. Then on November 15 Pike thought he saw a mountain in the distance; looking through a spyglass, he was certain it was a mountain. He showed it to Dr. Robinson, but said nothing more until half an hour later when they reached the top of a small hill and definitely saw mountains ahead. As the rest of the party, who were following behind them, came up onto the hill "they with one accord gave three cheers to the Mexican mountains." Still following the trail of the Spanish cavalry, they continued westward. One of their horses died and its load had to be distributed among the other weary animals.

On the 22nd, they met a Pawnee war party returning from an unsuccessful search for enemies. The sixty warriors, who were frustrated and in a bad mood, at first behaved with reasonable friendliness, but quickly they began to steal any small objects they could lay hands on, even trying to take away the pistols that Pike wore. Finally Pike ordered his men to separate themselves from the Indians and announced that he would kill the first warrior who touched their baggage. Immediately the Indians began to move away.

A day later, Pike decided to leave most of his men at a good place and to try himself to reach the high point of the "blue mountain" — what today is called Pike's Peak. He had the party build a breastwork of logs five feet high, forming three walls with a river on the fourth side, and place all the baggage in it. That, he felt, would allow his men to hold off any other stray war party that might happen along. Then he, Dr. Robinson, and two soldiers struck out toward the mountain. Three days later they reached the top of what now is Cheyenne Mountain. The Grand Peak, as the lieutenant referred to it, was still some fifteen or sixteen miles away and considerably higher. Their cotton uniforms were much too light for the cold weather and it had begun to snow heavily, so he decided to go no farther. That was the closest Pike ever came to the peak later named for him. They turned around and struggled back to their last campsite, "where we all four made a meal on one partridge and a piece of deer's ribs the ravens had left us, being the first we had eaten in that forty-eight hours."

They returned to the rest of the party, finding that all was well; the snow continued, but next day they moved ahead fifteen miles. The following day the snow was so heavy they remained in camp. Their horses had to paw it away to reach the meager grass and were further tormented by birds that were so hungry they landed on the horses' backs and pecked at their sores.

In the mountains, Pike lost the trail of the Spanish force and decided to bear southwest. His little group struggled through bad weather and difficult passes. On December 25, they kept to their camp all day and Pike noted

> Here, 800 miles from the frontier of our country, in the most inclement season of the year, not one person clothed for the winter, many without blankets (having been obliged to cut them up for socks, etc.), and now lying down at night on the snow or wet ground, one side burning whilst the other was

pierced with the cold wind — this was in part the situation of the party, whilst some were endeavoring to make a miserable substitute of raw buffalo hide for shoes, etc. I will not speak of diet, as I conceive that to be beneath the serious consideration of a man on a voyage of such nature.

Early in January Pike decided to build a stockade, leave the worn-out horses and most of the baggage in it, with the interpreter and one soldier in charge, and to take the rest of the party ahead on foot, carrying what they could on their backs. On they went. The night of the 17th the temperature was about ten degrees below zero and the feet of nine men, including both of the hunters, were frozen. Some of the men had to be left there and the remainder struggled ahead.

Toward the end of the month, they reached the upper part of the Rio Grande River. Pike and Robinson knew then that they were close to Spanish territory and they began to think of what they should do next. Conditions had been strained between the United States and Spain when they left St. Louis; what if the two countries were now at war? The little party set to work to build a log blockhouse, which Pike felt they would be able to defend against a considerably larger force. The lieutenant dispatched his sergeant back along their trail to pick up all the men left behind and to bring them in. Then Dr. Robinson, who carried papers that showed that he had a supposedly legitimate debt to collect from a resident of Santa Fe, set off by himself toward that city.

Pike and his men soon were taken into custody by the Spanish authorities, but they were treated well. In due course, Pike was questioned by Salcedo, the captain-general, at his headquarters in Chihuahua. Most of Pike's papers and his sextant were confiscated. There is no record of any conferences Robinson may have had with Salcedo or other officials, but it seems that there must have been such conferences. Then they were escorted to Natochitoches, in United States territory, and released. On July 1 they reached the military post there, Fort Claiborne, where they were thrilled to see the American flag flying overhead.

Despite the loss of some of Pike's notes, he had kept others, including his journal, and was able to reconstruct a map of the area he had passed through; the information that he brought back was the first the United States knew about a large part of the Louisiana Purchase and the best they would know about the Southwest for some years to come. Pike and his companions had struggled bravely to obtain that information — and also apparently to get Dr. Robinson to Mexico. But just why the doctor had to get there still remains a mystery.

Burr Acts

The growing difficulties with Spanish forces in Texas and the resulting public indignation against Spain in the United States was made to order for Aaron Burr, and he renewed his efforts to detach Louisiana from the United States and use it as a springboard for a Mexican take-over. In 1806, as Pike was starting out on his journey of exploration, Burr gathered a staff of conspirators and sent representatives to New Orleans to keep him informed of developments there. Wilkinson, not wanting to be identified with Burr's schemes now that they were becoming such open knowledge, had not written to the former vice president for some months. Jonathan Dayton, a long-time friend of Burr's, undertook to bring Wilkinson back into Burr's fold. The general directly controlled most of the Louisiana Purchase by virtue of his position as governor of Louisiana Territory and indirectly controlled the remainder of it — the Territory of Orleans — through his position of Commander-in-Chief of the Army. If Louisiana were to be split away from the Union, Wilkinson's help would be essential.

Dayton wrote a prodding letter to Wilkinson in which he told him that President Jefferson had decided to replace him. "Jefferson will affect to yield reluctantly to the public sentiment, but yield he will. Prepare yourself, therefore, for it. You know the rest. You are not a man to despair, or even despond, especially when such prospects offer in another quarter. Are you ready? Are your numerous associates ready? Wealth and Glory! Louisiana and Mexico!" That, Dayton thought, gave Wilkinson no choice but to join the conspirators.

A couple of days later, Burr wrote a letter in cipher to Wilkinson, giving many of his plans. By autumn, he said, he would be able to move down the Ohio and Mississippi with as many as a thousand men in boats. By mid-December he would meet Wilkinson at Natchez to decide just where they would strike first. Although Burr did not say so precisely, it seemed obvious that New Orleans would be the first city to fall.

By late August, 1806, Burr was at Blennerhassett's Island in the Ohio River. Its owner, Harman Blennerhassett, had become his staunch supporter and the island was turned into a staging area for Burr's expedition. Having seen to it that the boats that were being built and the men that were being recruited could assemble there, Burr continued downstream, gathering men, money, and supplies as he went — and stirring up constant rumors that found their way back to President Jefferson. Toward the end of October, the president wrote to the authorities in the states and territories bordering the Ohio and Mississippi rivers, telling them to watch Burr and to arrest him if he made any overt move.

Also late in October, Wilkinson decided to act; if he became the savior of the Union, the president could hardly remove him from his post. Therefore he wrote to Jefferson, telling him of Burr's plans in highly dramatic language, and at the same time alerted the military posts under his command to guard against attack. He also wrote to the Spanish authorities, warning them that there was a move afoot by some Americans to take over Spanish territory, but that he was doing his best to prevent it — and that he expected to be paid well for his efforts. Wilkinson, as commander of all United States Army troops, then went to New Orleans and sounded the alarm against the attack, calling out the militia, building fortifications, and arresting those citizens who might oppose him. This largely trumped-up emergency gave him the chance to imprison or ship out, not only from New Orleans but from the whole western area, both his enemies and his old friends who knew too much about him.

As Burr progressed downriver, however, his conspiracy

began to fall apart. He was investigated by a grand jury in Kentucky, but not indicted. Some of his boats were seized, and Blennerhassett's Island was raided and vandalized by a posse. His progress was so delayed that he did not reach Mississippi until January of 1807, and there he was again arrested and brought before a grand jury.

Once again the jury failed to indict him, but it had become obvious that his plans were ruined; some of his people had deserted him and by this time an antagonistic Wilkinson awaited him at New Orleans. While still technically under arrest in Mississippi he fled toward Mobile, which was in Spanish territory, but he was apprehended by United States authorities near Fort Stoddard, Alabama.

Aaron Burr gathering men along the Ohio River. He hoped to detach Louisiana from the United States with their aid.

The Trials

Burr was brought first by the federal government before a grand jury in Richmond, Virginia. Chief Justice John Marshall presided. Wilkinson was the star witness for the prosecution, and the code letter from Burr was his main piece of evidence. Burr, clad in black silk and a powdered wig, faced Wilkinson in his brightly colored uniform. The former vice president, himself an attorney, had retained four skillful lawyers to defend him.

Wilkinson was several times forced to contradict himself as well as to admit that he had badly decoded the key letter and had omitted parts of it that might implicate him; and he also had to admit that he had known, corresponded with, and visited Burr over a period of some years. At one point an attempt was even made to have the jury indict Wilkinson for treason, but it failed. Eventually, however, Burr was indicted for treason.

The trial itself, three months later, was largely a rerun of the grand jury proceedings, with Wilkinson again the chief witness and the defense again trying, with some success, to make him look like the chief villain. Marshall again presided. Burr was found "not guilty." The main reasons for this finding were Marshall's interpretations that two witnesses were necessary to prove treason and that as far as the admissible evidence went, Burr's plans had not progressed far enough for him actually to have committed the offense. The verdict infuriated President Jefferson and helped to start a feud between the president and the chief justice. It also angered many private citizens, some of whom burned Burr and Marshall in effigy and marched angrily through the streets in protest. A third trial of Burr, for a misdemeanor in setting in motion an invasion of Spanish territory, followed much the same procedure; it lasted a week, and ended in another "not guilty" finding.

But the end result of these trials, in addition to the notorious Burr-Hamilton duel, was to make Burr forever a villain in the minds of most Americans. The trials also raised a good many questions about General Wilkinson, who was, however, permitted to continue his dubious career.

The Results of
the Louisiana Purchase

The American historian Henry Adams put the results of purchasing Louisiana thus: "The annexation of Louisiana was an event so portentous as to defy measurement; it gave a new face to politics, and ranked in historical importance next to the Declaration of Independence and the adoption of the Constitution, — events of which it was the logical outcome; but as a matter of diplomacy it was unparalleled, because it cost almost nothing."

It did remake American politics. Up to that time, the Republican party, founded and led by Jefferson, had been the states'-rights party. Even so, Jefferson's purchase of this immense area — equal to the existing United States — without reference to those states was the greatest use of federal authority up to that time. The fact that such a move could be taken even by Jefferson, champion of the individual states, foretold that the authority of the states would dwindle and that of the central government would grow.

In the congressional debate that followed the Louisiana Purchase, every speaker agreed that the United States government had the power to acquire such new land; the differences came only in the way they thought it should be governed. As Adams also said, for the first time all parties agreed that the federal government could govern. Thus, the Louisiana Purchase indicated a major step in the growth of federal power in the United States.

In addition, the reports of the first explorers, once they were published, gave the country the first real information about what, up to that time, was really a blank area on the map. Such reports gave Americans information that made the Louisiana Purchase, and Oregon beyond, real and solid in the national mind. They described the geography and geology, the Indian tribes, the animals, and the plants. When Americans thought about the Louisiana Purchase now, they thought in terms of the descriptions made by Lewis, Clark, and Pike. Indeed, it was these two captains and the lieutenant who introduced this vast new territory to America.

The Louisiana Purchase also had a striking impact upon the thinking of the American people, upon their beliefs and attitudes — and this was perhaps the most important development of all. The political events and the new information turned the face of America westward. Until that time, Americans in many ways still had a colonial attitude; they still looked to England and to France. Now they looked carefully and hard at their own continent; for the first time, Americans became Americans as we know them, people with a continental view. It soon became a foregone conclusion that the United States would expand westward and the Louisiana Purchase provided the magnetic, unifying impetus behind expansion. It has also been said that the purchase made certain that the Civil War would not split the Union. Abraham Lincoln was among those who thought so, and he said of the American land, "In all its adaptations and aptitudes, it demands union and abhors separation."

But the purchase of Louisiana also set in motion other forces pulling in the opposite direction, though in the end they proved weaker. Some of them were personified in Wilkinson and Burr. More important, however, the purchase of Louisiana almost immediately opened the question of slavery in the new area and in that sense made certain there *would* be a Civil War. Federalist politicians from New England, imagining that much of the new land would become slave territory, threatened to secede from the United States rather than permit their section of the country to be so outnumbered. Actually, this was a great deal more a matter of sectional competition than of humanitarian interest in the slaves themselves; what the New Englanders feared was that the uneasy balance between the mercantile states of the North and their agrarian, slave-holding rivals, would be tipped in favor of the latter. When secession did come later, it of course was precipitated by the South, and for almost exactly the opposite reason; the South wanted to establish control over some of the new western territories and the bulk of the nation opposed it. While there certainly were other reasons for the outbreak of the American Civil War, this particular one led to outright guerrilla warfare in Kansas, which in turn helped to trigger the larger war.

Moreover, the Louisiana Purchase, by doubling the area of the country, also made the United States strong enough to withstand almost any outside military attack conceivable in the nineteenth century. In this way, it gave the new country an opportunity to develop, free of the threats that had surrounded it up to that time. Thus it was the United States that soon, in 1812, felt able to declare war on Britain and to try to seize Canada. While this probably was not a wise move, it nevertheless indicated the new temper of the country.

In a broader sense the purchase also insured that Americans would truly develop into a separate people and not simply dissident Britons. Before long, the vast new spaces were to draw immigrants from most of the other countries of Europe. The Scandinavians, the Germans, and the later arrivals from other countries had their own traditions and their own ties with foreign lands. When they began to mix with the descendents of the original settlers, the modern social organization of the United States started to emerge. Indeed it is noteworthy that during the Civial War the ranks of the Union army were filled with men of varied immigrant background.

Unfortunately, the purchase of Louisiana insured the tragic fate of the Indian nations. If Americans of European background were to take over the land, the first Americans to live there had little chance to remain. Lewis, Clark, and Pike treated the Indians fairly, honestly, and with respect; as a result, most of the western tribes they met remained friendly to the United States until cheated or otherwise mistreated by white men who came later. Lewis met his untimely death a very few years after returning from the expedition, but Clark long remained a friend of the Indians. Unlike most white men of the day, Clark liked them. When tribesmen came to St. Louis, they visited Clark first; and United States government or commercial groups heading west sought his advice. On occasion the government used him as a good-will ambassador to the Indian nations, and he seems always to have been able both to get the Indians to cooperate and to obtain better treatment for them. Yet such first explorers as Clark were tolerant and unusual men in a number of ways; those who followed lacked many of their qualities and particularly their attitudes toward the original inhabitants of the territory.

Acquisition of Louisiana did not originate the philosophy of "manifest destiny," the idea that it was the obvious right and duty of the United States to own and settle the continent — but it gave that philosophy the push that carried it successfully forward. It gave Americans the United States that they know today — a group of states that is a single political unit, a country of Americans most of whose ancestors came from Europe; a country that spans a continent.

Bibliography

Abernethy, Thomas Perkins. *The Burr Conspiracy*. New York: Oxford University Press, 1954.

Adams, Henry. *History of the United States of America During the Administration of Thomas Jefferson*. Two volumes. New York: Albert and Charles Boni, 1930.

Barbé-Marbois, François. *Histoire de la Louisiane*. Paris: Firmin Didot, 1829.

Brown, Everett Somerville. *The Constitutional History of the Louisiana Purchase*. Berkeley: University of California Press, 1920.

Davis, Samuel M. "Some of the Consequences of the Louisiana Purchase," *Annual Report of the American Historical Association*, 1897.

DeVoto, Bernard. *The Course of Empire*. Boston: Houghton Mifflin Company, 1952.

————, editor. *The Journals of Lewis and Clark*. Boston: Houghton Mifflin Company, 1953.

Dufour, Charles L. *Ten Flags in the Wind*. New York: Harper & Row, 1967.

Fortier, Alcée. *A History of Louisiana*. Four volumes. New York: Manzi, Joyant & Co., 1904.

Galloway, Bishop Chas. B. "Aaron Burr in Mississippi," *Publications of the Mississippi Historical Society*, X (1909).

Gass, Patrick. *Lewis and Clarke's Journal to the Rocky Mountains*. Dayton: Ells, Claflin, & Co., 1874.

Green, Thomas Marshall. *The Spanish Conspiracy*. Cincinnati: Robert Clarke & Co., 1891.

Hay, Thomas Robinson, and M. R. Werner. *The Admirable Trumpeter*. Garden City, N.Y.: Doubleday, Doran & Company, Inc., 1941.

Hosmer, James K. *The History of the Louisiana Purchase*. New York: D. Appleton and Company, 1902.

Howard, James Q. *History of the Louisiana Purchase*. Chicago: Callaghan & Company, 1902.

Jackson, Donald, editor. *Letters of the Lewis and Clark Expedition*. Urbana: University of Illinois Press, 1962.

Jacobs, James Ripley. *Tarnished Warrior*. New York: The Macmillan Company, 1938.

Marshall, Thomas Maitland. *A History of the Western Boundary of the Louisiana Purchase*. Berkeley: University of California Press, 1914.

McCaleb, Walter Flavius. "The Aaron Burr Conspiracy and New Orleans," *Annual Report of the American Historical Association*, 1903, I.

Parsons, Edward Alexander, editor. "The Letters of Robert R. Livingston," *Proceedings of the American Antiquarian Society*, LII (April 15, 1942–October 21, 1942).

Quaife, Milo Milton, editor. *The Journals of Captain Meriwether Lewis and Sergeant John Ordway*. Madison: The State Historical Society of Wisconsin, 1916.

_____, editor. *The Southwestern Expedition of Zebulon M. Pike*. Chicago: The Lakeside Press, 1925.

Sloane, William M. "The World Aspects of the Louisiana Purchase," *Annual Report of the American Historical Association*, 1903, I.

U.S. Government. *State Papers and Correspondence Bearing Upon the Purchase of the Territory of Louisiana*. Washington: Government Printing Office, 1903.

Van Doren, Mark, editor. *Correspondence of Aaron Burr and his Daughter, Theodosia*. New York: Covici-Friede Incorporated, 1929.

Walker, Francis A. *The Making of the Nation, 1783–1817*. New York: Charles Scribner's Sons, 1904.

Wandell, Samuel H., and Meade Minnigerode. *Aaron Burr*. Two volumes. New York; G. P. Putnam's Sons, 1925.

Index

About the Author

James P. Barry, a 1940 graduate of Ohio State University (cum laude, with distinction, Phi Beta Kappa), has been a career army officer, a university administrator, and an editor. He has written a number of books and articles on historical subjects, including three others in the Focus Books series. He also has done both the writing and photography for a recent picture book on the Great Lakes, *The Fate of the Lakes*. Mr. Barry is a resident of Columbus, Ohio, and is married to a high-school librarian.

11/16
4
No last date

11/27/23
4
N.L.O.